SEE A PLANT GROW!

PUMPKIN

by Charlie W. Sterling

TABLE OF CONTENTS

tadpole books

WORDS TO KNOW

flower

plant

pumpkin

seeds

shoot

vine

PUMPKIN

These are seeds.

seed

We plant one.

We water it.

I see a shoot!

The sun helps it grow.

I see a vine.

I see a flower!

A pumpkin grows!

It turns orange.

It grows big!

LET'S REVIEW!

Pumpkins start as seeds. They grow in stages. What color will this pumpkin turn?

INDEX